Editor

Erica N. Russikoff, M.A.

Contributing Editor

Christine Smith

Illustrators

Mark Mason

Renée Christine Yates

Cover Artist

Tony Carrillo

Editor in Chief

Ina Massler Levin, M.A.

Creative Director

Karen J. Goldfluss, M.S. Ed.

Imaging

Rosa C. See

Publisher

Mary D. Smith, M.S. Ed.

TCR 8840

Summertime Learning

Prepare Your Child for Kindergarten

With 8 weeks worth of reading, writing, math and just plain fun!

Includes over 300 stickers!

Teacher Created Resources

Teacher Created Resources, Inc.

6421 Industry Way

Westminster, CA 92683

www.teachercreated.com

ISBN: 978-1-4206-8840-5

© 2010 Teacher Created Resources, Inc.

Reprinted, 2011 (PO4553)

Made in U.S.A.

Teacher Created Resources

Table of Contents

Monday	Math: *Shining Stars*	
	Reading: *Sound Matching*	
Tuesday	Math: *Construction Count*	
	Writing: *Alphabet Train*	
Wednesday	Math: *Sky-High Numbers*	
	Reading: *Beginning Sounds*	
Thursday	Math: *Spotty Fun*	
	Writing: *Parts of a Story*	
Friday	Friday Fun: *Follow the Letters, Same and Different*	

Monday	Math: *Cross It Out*	
	Writing: *Alpha-Clothing*	
Tuesday	Math: *Dots All Around*	
	Reading: *Pond Pals*	
Wednesday	Math: *Small and Big*	
	Writing: *Sand Castle*	
Thursday	Math: *On the Road*	
	Reading: *Writing Words*	
Friday	Friday Fun: *What's Missing?, Blast Off*	

Monday	Math: *Say Cheese!*	
	Reading: *Same Ending Sound*	
Tuesday	Math: *Fish Counting*	
	Writing: *What I Like to Do*	
Wednesday	Math: *What Comes Next?*	
	Reading: *Doesn't Belong*	
Thursday	Math: *Guess and Count*	
	Writing: *All Mixed Up*	
Friday	Friday Fun: *Who I Am, Pizza*	

Monday	Math: *Adding Buttons*	
	Writing: *Shell Pairs*	
Tuesday	Math: *Holds the Most*	
	Reading: *Add an Ending Sound*	
Wednesday	Math: *Fish Bowl Math*	
	Writing: *My Friend*	
Thursday	Math: *Show and Tell*	
	Reading: *Color Words*	
Friday	Friday Fun: *Draw a Bird, Flower Needs*	

Monday	Math: *Animal Subtraction*	
	Reading: *In the Kitchen*	
Tuesday	Math: *Sounds and Sizes*	
	Writing: *Make a Wish*	
Wednesday	Math: *On the Go*	
	Reading: *Animal Names*	

Table of Contents (cont.)

Dear Parents,

Did you know that all young people experience learning losses when they don't engage in educational activities during the summer? That means some of what they've spent time learning over the preceding school year evaporates during the summer months. However, summer learning loss *is* something that you can help prevent. Summer is the perfect time for fun and engaging activities that can help children maintain and grow their academic skills. Here are just a few:

☼ Read with your child every day. Visit your local library together, and select books on subjects that interest your child.

☼ Ask your child's teacher for recommendations of books for summer reading. The Summer Reading List in this publication is a good start.

☼ Explore parks, nature preserves, museums, and cultural centers.

☼ Consider every day as a day full of teachable moments. Measuring in recipes and reviewing maps before a car trip are ways to learn or reinforce a skill. Use the Learning Experiences in the back of this book for more ideas.

☼ Each day, set goals to accomplish. For example, do five math problems or read a chapter in a book.

☼ Encourage your child to complete the activities in books, such as *Summertime Learning*, to help bridge the summer learning gap.

Our vision is for every child to be safe, healthy, and engaged in learning during the summer. Learn more at *www.summerlearning.org* and *www.summerlearningcampaign.org*.

Have a *memorable* summer!

Ron Fairchild
Chief Executive Officer
National Summer Learning Association

How to Use This Book

As a parent, you know that summertime is a time for fun and learning. So it is quite useful that fun and learning can go hand in hand when your child uses *Summertime Learning*.

There are many ways to use this book effectively with your child. We list three ideas on page 6. (See "Day by Day," "Pick and Choose," and "All of a Kind.") You may choose one way on one day, and, on another day, choose something else.

Book Organization

Summertime Learning is organized around an eight-week summer vacation period. For each weekday, there are two lessons. Each Monday through Thursday, there is a math lesson. Additionally, during the odd-numbered weeks, there is a reading lesson on Monday and Wednesday and a writing lesson on Tuesday and Thursday. During the even-numbered weeks, these lessons switch days. (Reading lessons are on Tuesday and Thursday, and writing lessons are on Monday and Wednesday.) Friday features two Friday Fun activities (one typically being a puzzle). The calendar looks like this:

Day	Week 1	Week 2	Week 3	Week 4	Week 5	Week 6	Week 7	Week 8
M	Math --- Reading	Math --- Writing	Math --- Reading	Math --- Writing	Math --- Reading	Math --- Writing	Math --- Reading	Math --- Writing
T	Math --- Writing	Math --- Reading	Math --- Writing	Math --- Reading	Math --- Writing	Math --- Reading	Math --- Writing	Math --- Reading
W	Math --- Reading	Math --- Writing	Math --- Reading	Math --- Writing	Math --- Reading	Math --- Writing	Math --- Reading	Math --- Writing
Th	Math --- Writing	Math --- Reading	Math --- Writing	Math --- Reading	Math --- Writing	Math --- Reading	Math --- Writing	Math --- Reading
F	Friday Fun --- Friday Fun	Friday Fun --- Friday Fun	Friday Fun --- Friday Fun	Friday Fun --- Friday Fun	Friday Fun --- Friday Fun	Friday Fun --- Friday Fun	Friday Fun --- Friday Fun	Friday Fun --- Friday Fun

How to Use This Book
(cont.)

Day by Day

You can have your child do the activities in order, beginning on the first Monday of summer vacation. He or she can complete the two lessons provided for each day. It does not matter if math, reading, or writing is completed first. The pages are designed so that each day of the week's lessons are back to back. The book is also perforated. This gives you the option of tearing the pages out for your child to work on. If you opt to have your child tear out the pages, you might want to store the completed pages in a special folder or three-ring binder that your child decorates.

Pick and Choose

You may find that you do not want to have your child work strictly in order. Feel free to pick and choose any combination of pages based on your child's needs and interests.

All of a Kind

Perhaps your child needs more help in one area than another. You may opt to have him or her work only on math, reading, or writing.

Keeping Track

A Reward Chart is included on page 10 of this book, so you and your child can keep track of the activities that have been completed. This page is designed to be used with the stickers provided. Once your child has finished a page, have him or her put a sticker on the castle. If you don't want to use stickers for this, have your child color in a circle each time an activity is completed.

The stickers can also be used on the individual pages. As your child finishes a page, let him or her place a sticker in the sun at the top of the page. If he or she asks where to begin the next day, simply have him or her start on the page after the last sticker.

There are enough stickers to use for both the Reward Chart and the sun on each page. Plus, there are extra stickers for your child to enjoy.

Standards and Skills

Each activity in *Summertime Learning* meets one or more of the following standards and skills*. The activities in this book are designed to help your child reinforce the skills learned during preschool, as well as introduce new skills that will be learned in kindergarten.

Language Arts Standards

- ✿ Uses the general skills and strategies of the writing process
- ✿ Uses the stylistic and rhetorical aspects of writing
- ✿ Uses grammatical and mechanical conventions in written compositions
- ✿ Gathers and uses information for research purposes
- ✿ Uses the general skills and strategies of the reading process
- ✿ Uses reading skills and strategies to understand and interpret a variety of literary texts
- ✿ Uses reading skills and strategies to understand a variety of informational texts
- ✿ Uses listening and speaking strategies for different purposes
- ✿ Uses viewing skills and strategies to understand and interpret visual media
- ✿ Understands the characteristics and components of the media

Mathematics Standards

- ✿ Uses a variety of strategies in the problem-solving process
- ✿ Understands and applies basic and advanced properties of the concepts of numbers
- ✿ Uses basic and advanced procedures while performing the processes of computation
- ✿ Understands and applies basic and advanced properties of the concepts of measurement
- ✿ Understands and applies basic and advanced properties of the concepts of geometry
- ✿ Understands and applies basic and advanced concepts of statistics and data analysis
- ✿ Understands and applies basic and advanced concepts of probability
- ✿ Understands and applies basic and advanced properties of functions and algebra

Writing Skills

- ✿ Knows that pictures, letters, and words communicate information
- ✿ Uses drawings to express thoughts, feelings, and ideas
- ✿ Uses forms of emergent writing for a variety of purposes
- ✿ Dictates stories, poems, and personal narratives
- ✿ Uses knowledge of letters to write familiar words, such as own name
- ✿ Uses writing tools and materials

Standards and Skills
(cont.)

Writing Skills *(cont.)*

- ✿ Organizes written work
- ✿ Uses basic rules of grammar
- ✿ Uses phonic knowledge to spell simple words
- ✿ Uses upper- and lowercase letters of the alphabet, spaces words and sentences, writes from left-to-right and top-to-bottom
- ✿ Uses complete sentences
- ✿ Uses nouns, verbs, and adjectives
- ✿ Knows to capitalize names and the first words of a sentence
- ✿ Uses periods at the end of sentences

Reading Skills

- ✿ Understands the differences between letters, numbers, and words and knows the significance of spaces between words
- ✿ Understands that illustrations and pictures convey meaning
- ✿ Knows the proper way to handle books
- ✿ Knows that print is read from left-to-right, top-to-bottom, and that books are read front-to-back
- ✿ Knows some letters of the alphabet, such as those in the student's own name
- ✿ Knows some familiar words in print, such as own first name
- ✿ Uses visual and verbal cues, including pictures, to comprehend new words and stories
- ✿ Uses phonetic analysis to decode unknown words
- ✿ Knows the sequence of events in a story
- ✿ Uses reading skills and strategies to understand and interpret a variety of literary and informational texts
- ✿ Summarizes information found in texts

Listening Skills

- ✿ Listens for a variety of purposes
- ✿ Follows one- and two-step directions
- ✿ Knows rhyming sounds and simple rhymes
- ✿ Knows that words are made up of sounds
- ✿ Listens to a variety of fiction, nonfiction, poetry, drama, rhymes, and songs

Mathematics Skills

- Draws pictures to represent problems
- Explains to others how she or he solved a numerical problem
- Understands that numbers represent the quantity of objects
- Counts by ones to ten or higher
- Counts objects
- Knows the written numerals 0–9 and that they represent quantities
- Compares the quantity of objects
- Understands symbolic, concrete, and pictorial representations of numbers
- Knows that the quantity of objects can change by adding or taking away objects
- Adds and subtracts whole numbers
- Estimates quantities
- Can identify objects in a set as smallest/largest, lightest/heaviest, shortest/longest
- Knows and uses descriptive terms of measurement
- Knows that different-sized containers will hold more or less
- Understands the basic measures length, width, height, weight, and temperature
- Understands the concept of time and how it is measured
- Knows how to measure length and temperature
- Can identify basic shapes
- Knows how to describe position and location
- Sorts and groups objects by attributes
- Recognizes, extends, and creates patterns using shapes, objects, and numbers
- Knows that graphs represent information

* Standards and Skills used with permission from McREL (Copyright 2009, McREL. Midcontinent Research for Education and Learning. Address: 4601 DTC Boulevard, Suite 500, Denver, CO 80237. Telephone: 303-337-0990. Web site: www.mcrel.org/standards-benchmarks)

Reward Chart

10

Shining Stars

Directions: Color the correct number of stars in each row.

0	☆ ☆ ☆ ☆ ☆ ☆ ☆ ☆ ☆ ☆
1	☆ ☆ ☆ ☆ ☆ ☆ ☆ ☆ ☆ ☆
2	☆ ☆ ☆ ☆ ☆ ☆ ☆ ☆ ☆ ☆
3	☆ ☆ ☆ ☆ ☆ ☆ ☆ ☆ ☆ ☆
4	☆ ☆ ☆ ☆ ☆ ☆ ☆ ☆ ☆ ☆
5	☆ ☆ ☆ ☆ ☆ ☆ ☆ ☆ ☆ ☆
6	☆ ☆ ☆ ☆ ☆ ☆ ☆ ☆ ☆ ☆
7	☆ ☆ ☆ ☆ ☆ ☆ ☆ ☆ ☆ ☆
8	☆ ☆ ☆ ☆ ☆ ☆ ☆ ☆ ☆ ☆
9	☆ ☆ ☆ ☆ ☆ ☆ ☆ ☆ ☆ ☆
10	☆ ☆ ☆ ☆ ☆ ☆ ☆ ☆ ☆ ☆

Sound Matching

Directions: Color the pictures in each row that begin with the letter shown.

1. **B**	
2. **L**	
3. **M**	
4. **R**	
5. **S**	

Construction Count

Directions: Count the objects. Write the correct number in each box.

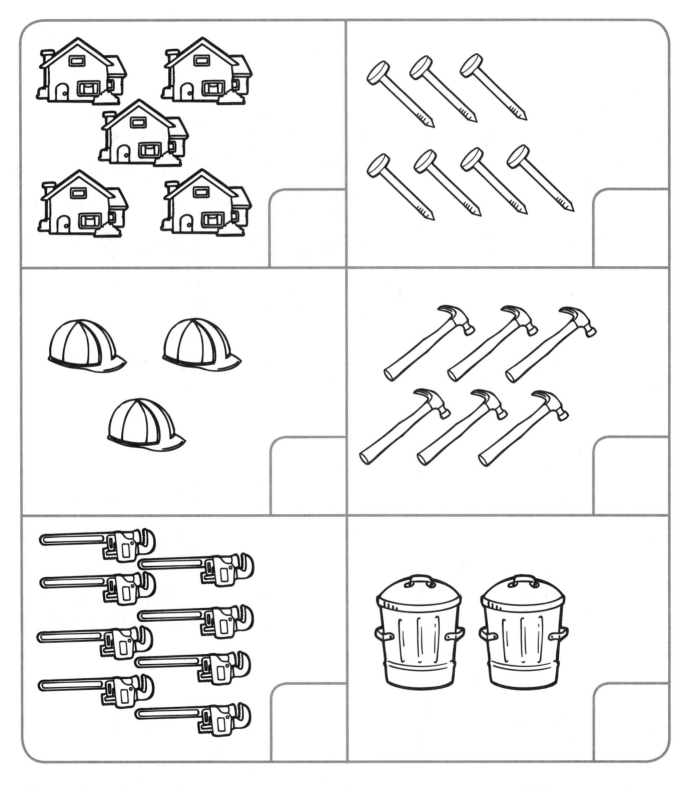

Alphabet Train

Directions: Fill in the missing uppercase letters of the alphabet.

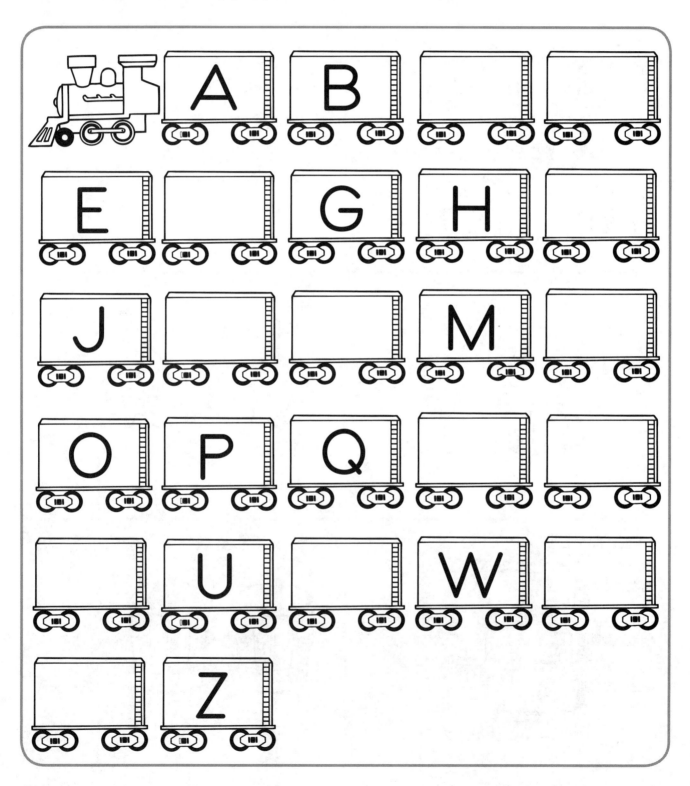

Sky-High Numbers

Directions: Write the missing numbers on each cloud to show how you count from 1 to 9.

___ 2 3 4 ___ ___ ___ 8 9

1 ___ ___ ___ 5 6 7 ___ 9

1 2 3 ___ 5 ___ 7 ___ ___

Beginning Sounds

Directions: Say the name of each picture. Fill in the bubble that shows the letter for the beginning sound.

1.	2.	3.
○ ○ ○	○ ○ ○	○ ○ ○
c r l	f t b	c l m
4.	5.	6.
○ ○ ○	○ ○ ○	○ ○ ○
m d v	f n t	g w r
7.	8.	9.
○ ○ ○	○ ○ ○	○ ○ ○
s h r	s f j	k w t

Spotty Fun

Directions: Look at the number in each box. Add that number of spots to the animal. Color the animals.

Parts of a Story

Directions: Read a story. Illustrate the beginning, middle, and end of the story below.

Beginning

Middle

End

Follow the Letters

Directions: Start with the letter "A" and follow the letters of the alphabet to find the picture. Color the picture.

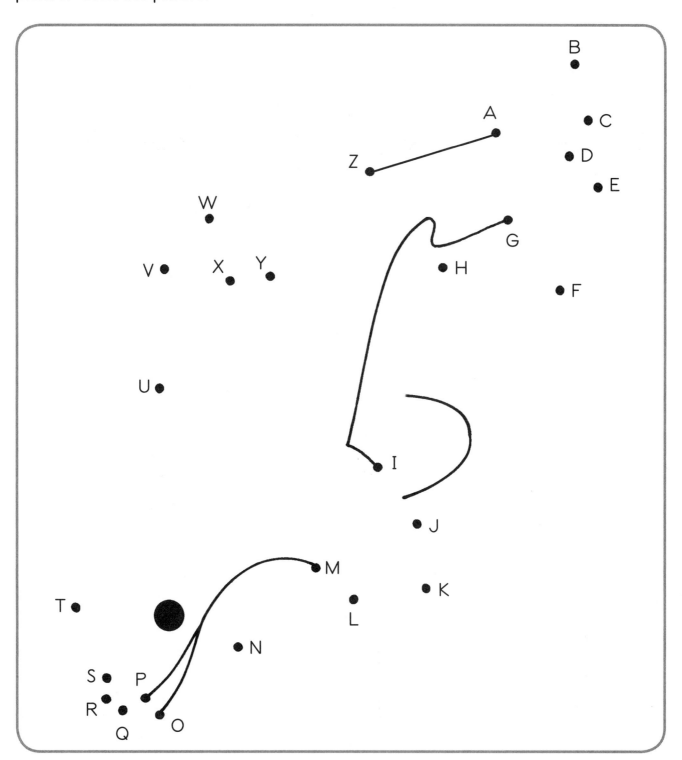

Same and Different

Directions: Look at the pictures in each row. Color the pictures in each row that are the same. Cross out the picture that is different.

Cross It Out

Directions: Look at each group of shapes. Put an **X** on the one that does not belong.

1.

2.

3.

4.

Alpha-Clothing

Writing

Directions: Follow the string and arrows, and fill in the missing lowercase letters of the alphabet.

22

©Teacher Created Resources, Inc.

Dots All Around

Directions: Count the number of dots on each ladybug. Write the number in the box.

1.

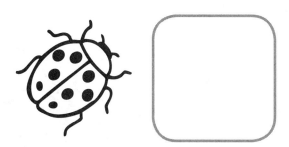

5.

2.

6.

3.

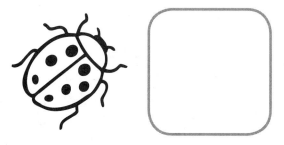

7.

4.

8.

Pond Pals

Directions: Look at the picture. Circle each animal or bug *beginning* with the /f/ sound. Draw a box around each animal *beginning* with the /r/ sound. Place an **X** over each animal or bug *beginning* with the /s/ sound.

Small and Big

Directions: Circle the small item in each box. Draw a square around the big item in each box. Color your favorite foods.

Sand Castle

Directions: Who lives in this sand castle? Draw a picture of him or her.

On the Road

Directions: Look at the list of items below. Count how many you can find in the picture, and write the number on the line next to the item. Color the picture.

How many can you find?

Writing Words

Directions: Add the beginning sound shown in the first box to each word in the row. Practice reading the words.

1. **t**

_____ op   _____ ub   _____ ire

2. **b**

_____ ag   _____ ell   _____ all

3. **r**

_____ ing   _____ ug   _____ ock

4. **p**

_____ ig   _____ ot   _____ en

What's Missing?

Directions: Draw in the missing part of each picture. Color the pictures.

bird

giraffe

rhino

dog

kangaroo

gorilla

Blast Off

Directions: Look at the two pictures below. Circle four things that are different in the second picture.

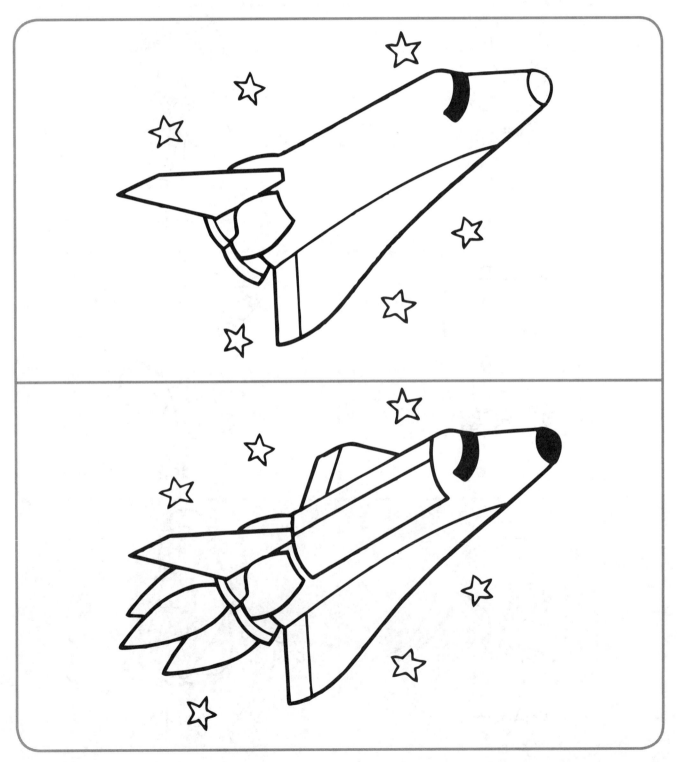

Say Cheese!

Directions: Use a yellow crayon to color the piece of cheese in each row that has the *most* holes. Cross out the piece of cheese with the *fewest* holes in each row.

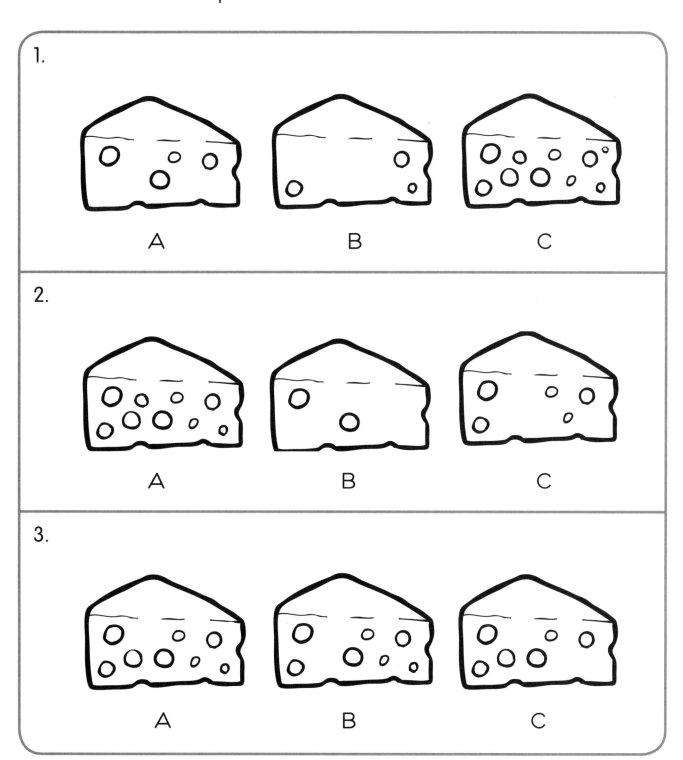

Same Ending Sound

Directions: Say the name of the picture in the first box. Color the pictures in that row that end with the same sound.

1. 6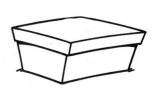

2.

3.

4.

5.

Fish Counting

Directions: Look at the number at the bottom right of each box. Draw that many bubbles for the fish.

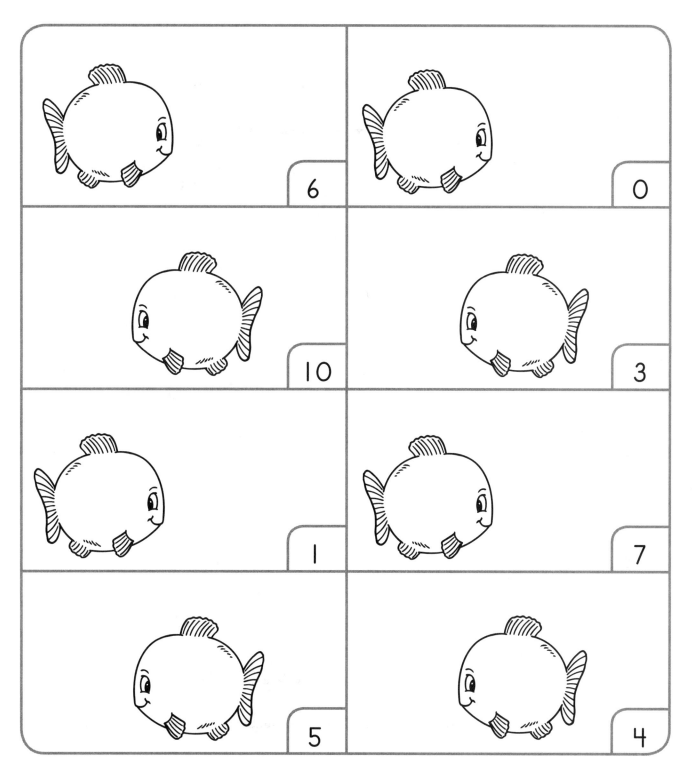

What I Like to Do

Directions: Finish the sentence below. Draw a picture to show what you like to do.

I like to_____ .

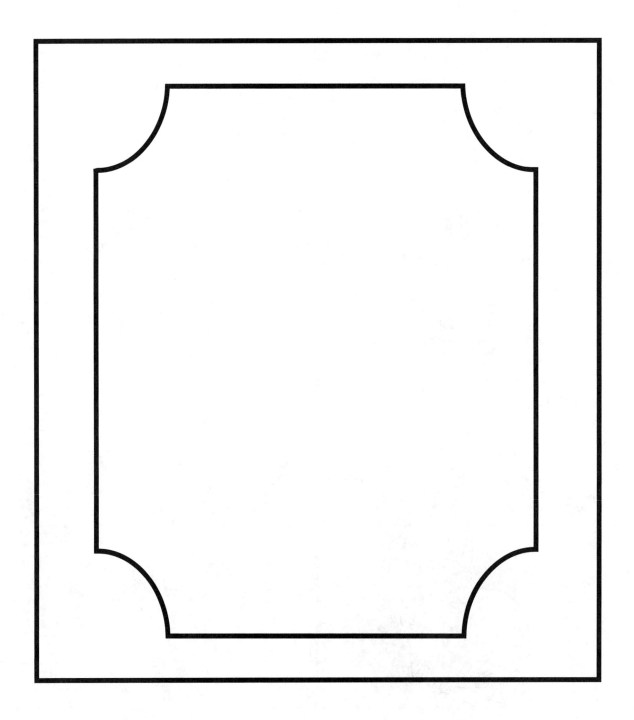

What Comes Next?

Directions: Look at the patterns below. Draw what comes next.

Doesn't Belong

Directions: Look at the pictures in each row. Say the name of each picture. Cross out the picture that does not end with the same sound as the other two pictures.

Guess and Count

Directions: Guess how many gumballs are in each machine, and write the number on the first line in the box. Then count the gumballs, and write the actual number on the second line.

1.

_____   _____
Guess   Count

4.

_____   _____
Guess   Count

2.

_____   _____
Guess   Count

5.

_____   _____
Guess   Count

3.

_____   _____
Guess   Count

6.

_____   _____
Guess   Count

All Mixed Up

Directions: Show the correct order in each row by writing the numbers 1, 2, and 3 in the boxes.

Who I Am

Directions: Draw a picture of yourself. Then, fill in the blanks about you.

With my 👄 , I like to

_____ .

With my ✋ , I like to

_____ .

With my 👁 , I like to

_____ .

With my 👃 , I like to

_____ .

With my 🦶 , I like to

_____ .

With my 👂 , I like to

_____ .

Pizza

Directions: Count the dots. Then, color the puzzle.

1 = red   **2** = brown   **3** = yellow   **4** = blue

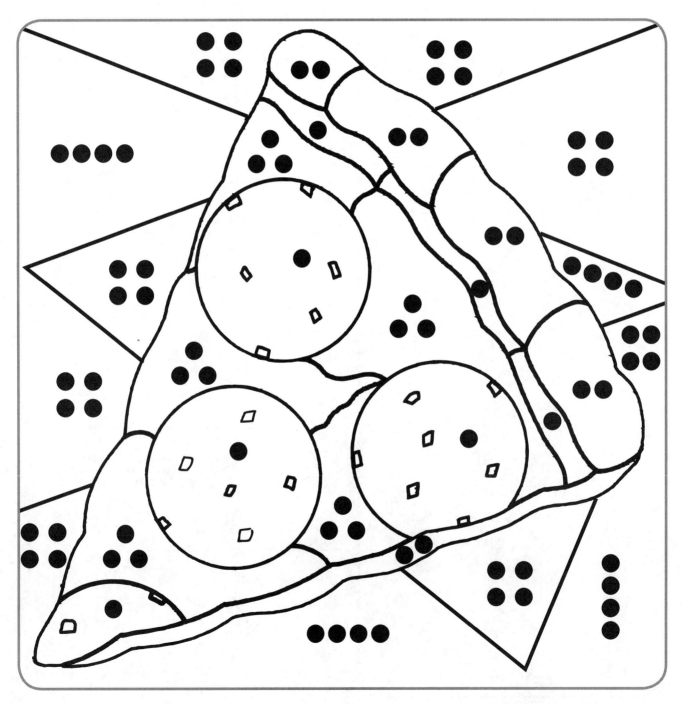

Adding Buttons

Directions: Look at the pictures. Add the buttons together to tell how many there are in all. Write the number in the box.

1.

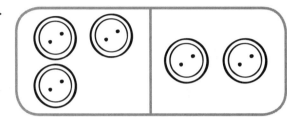

$$3 + 2 = \boxed{}$$

2.

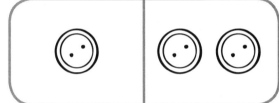

$$1 + 2 = \boxed{}$$

3.

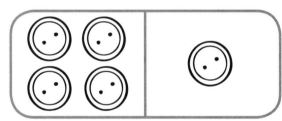

$$4 + 1 = \boxed{}$$

4.

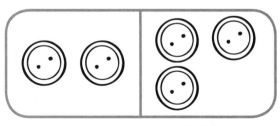

$$2 + 3 = \boxed{}$$

5.

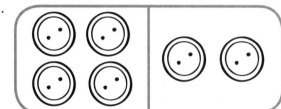

$$4 + 2 = \boxed{}$$

6.

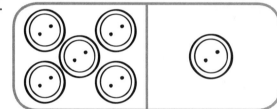

$$5 + 1 = \boxed{}$$

7.

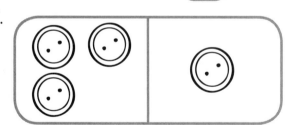

$$3 + 1 = \boxed{}$$

8.

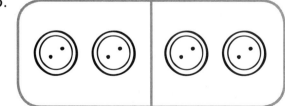

$$2 + 2 = \boxed{}$$

Shell Pairs

Directions: Match the uppercase and lowercase letters by coloring the shells the same color. Use a different color for each pair of shells.

Holds the Most

Directions: Look at each container. Color the container in each row that would hold the *most*.

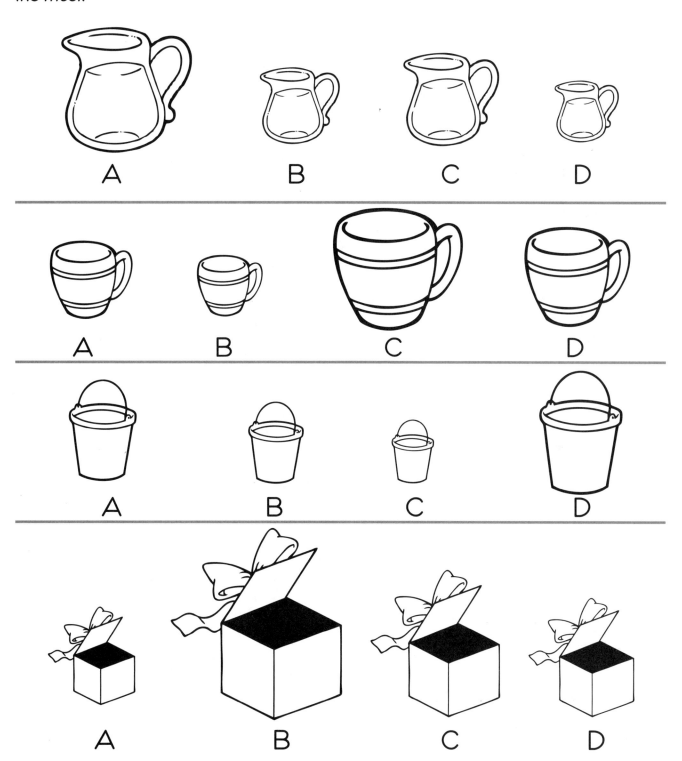

A   B   C   D

A   B   C   D

A   B   C   D

A   B   C   D

Add an Ending Sound

Directions: Say the name of each picture. Write the letter for its ending sound.

1.

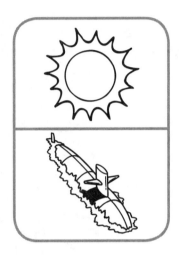

su____

su____

4.

ca____

ca____

2.

pi____

pi____

5.

do____

do____

3.

we____

we____

6.

ba____

ba____

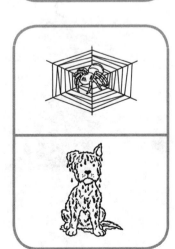

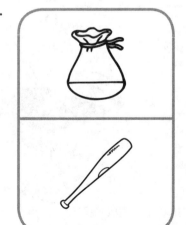

Fish Bowl Math

Directions: Draw fish in the two bowls to match the number story. Then, count how many fish there are altogether. Write the number in the circle.

$3 + 5 = $

$1 + 4 = $

$4 + 3 = $

Challenge: Practice addition by using dry beans or other small objects, such as buttons.

My Friend

Directions: Write about your friend. Draw a picture of your friend in the frame at the bottom of the page.

_____

is my friend.

My friend likes to eat _____

_____ .

My friend likes to play _____

_____ .

When we are together, we like to _____

_____ .

My friend is _____ years old.

My friend has _____ sisters

and _____ brothers.

I like my friend!

Show and Tell

Directions: Look at the graph to answer the questions.

☼ Which animal is shown most often? Circle that column.

☼ Which animal is shown least often? Color that column blue.

☼ Which animal is shown 3 times? Color that column yellow.

cats	dogs	rabbits
🐱	🐶	🐰
🐱		🐰
🐱		🐰
		🐰

Color Words

Directions: Trace the color words in each crayon. Color the crayon to match the color words.

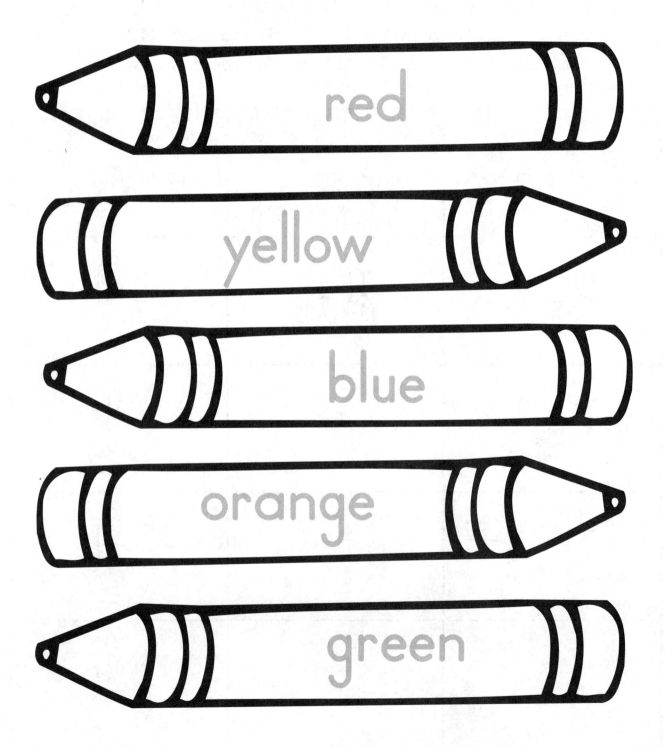

Draw a Bird

Directions: Use the numbered sequence to draw a bird in the box below. Add a background.

1	2	3
Draw a large oval. Draw a triangle in the center.	Add eyes and wings.	Draw a feather on the head. Add feet.

Flower Needs

Directions: Color the flower in the middle of the page. Color the pictures that show something that flowers need to live. Draw an **X** on the things that flowers do not need.

Animal Subtraction

Directions: Look at each picture. Write how many are left in each box.

1.

3 – 1 =

4.

2 – 1 =

2.

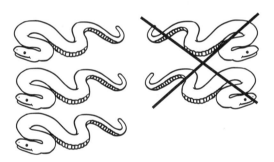

5 – 2 =

5.

3 – 2 =

3.

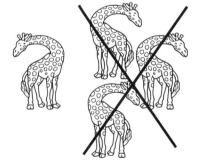

4 – 3 =

6.

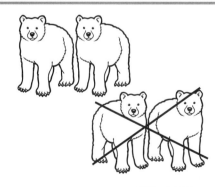

4 – 2 =

In the Kitchen

Directions: Color the food by following the instructions below. What letter do all of these foods start with? _____

☼ Color the  brown.

☼ Color the  yellow.

☼ Color the  red.

☼ Color the  green.

Sounds and Sizes

Directions: Label the musical instruments in each row with the letters **S** for small, **M** for medium, and **L** for large.

1.

_____   _____   _____

2.

_____   _____   _____

3.

_____   _____   _____

Directions: Read the sentence that goes with each picture. Trace the sentence.

I mix the cake.

Mom bakes the cake.

I frost the cake.

John makes a wish!

On the Go

Directions: Look at each picture. Write how many are left in each box.

1.

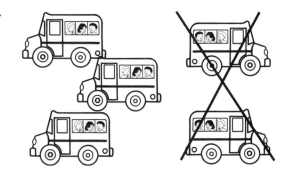

5 – 2= ☐

4.

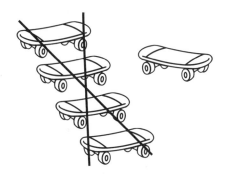

5 – 4= ☐

2.

6 – 4= ☐

5.

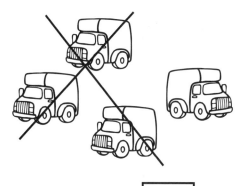

4 – 3= ☐

3.

5 – 3= ☐

6.

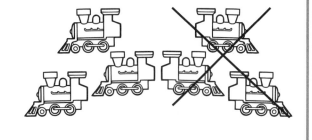

6 – 3= ☐

Animal Names

Directions: Read the animal names. Draw a line from the animal name to the picture of the animal.

dog

hen

cat

pig

bird

Shapes All Over

Directions: Count the different shapes. Write how many you find of each shape on the lines below.

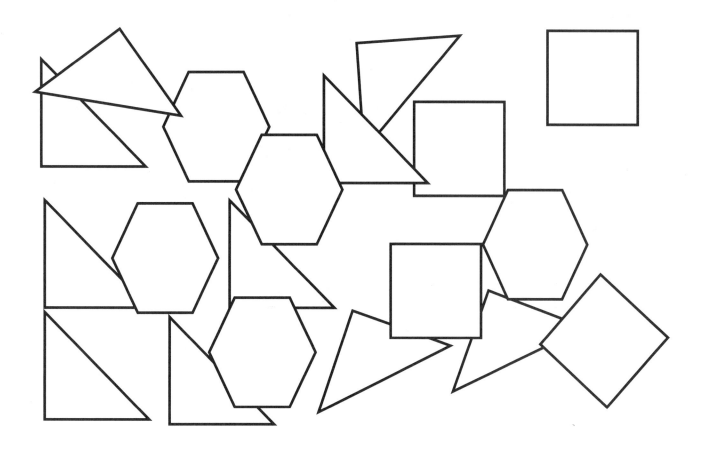

How many △ triangles? _____

How many ⬡ hexagons? _____

How many ☐ squares? _____

Colors

Directions: Complete each sentence with a word that tells more about the color. Draw pictures of what you wrote.

A _____ is red.

A _____ is blue.

A _____ is yellow.

A _____ is green.

How Big Am I?

Directions: Use a ruler or tape measure to help you fill in the blanks.

I am _____ feet tall.

My foot is _____ inches long.

My hand is _____ inches long.

Directions: Trace your hand in the box.
Then, follow the instructions below.

☼ Find your longest finger. Color it red.

☼ Find your shortest finger. Color it yellow.

☼ Measure your fingers. Write how long they are.

Rhyme or Not?

Directions: Say the names for each pair of pictures. Color the smiley face if the words rhyme. Color the sad face if the words do not rhyme.

1.

4.

2.

5.

3.

6.

Color the Squares

Directions: What numbers add together to make 10? Using a red and a blue crayon, color the squares **red** to match the first number. Then, color the rest of the squares **blue**. Count the blue squares, and write the number in the box.

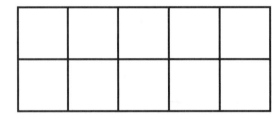

$$5 + \boxed{} = 10$$

$$2 + \boxed{} = 10$$

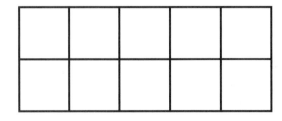

$$6 + \boxed{} = 10$$

$$10 + \boxed{} = 10$$

Picture Sentences

Week 6: Monday   Writing

Directions: Trace the sentence that describes the first picture. Practice writing it on your own. Then, trace and complete the sentence that describes the second picture.

The monkey swings.

The monkey

More and Less

Directions: Count the objects in each picture. Write the number in the box to the right. Compare the pictures. Color the picture with more objects. Draw an **X** on the picture with less objects.

1.

□ flowers

□ flowers

2.

□ apples

□ apples

3.

□ mushrooms

□ mushrooms

4.

□ dots

□ dots

Missing Vowel

Directions: Look at each picture. Say each word. Write the missing vowel on the line.

1.    c __ t

6. 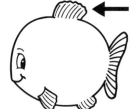   f __ n

2.    c __ t

7.    b __ g

3.    h __ g

8. 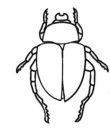   b __ g

4.    h __ g

9. 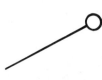   p __ n

5.    f __ n

10.    p __ n

About the Same

Directions: Look at the pictures in each row. Think about how much they would weigh if they were real. Color the two items in each row that would weigh about the same.

1.

2.

  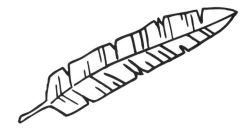

3.

4.

Four Seasons

Directions: Complete the sentence to tell about the four seasons. Draw a picture to match each season.

1.

In the fall, _____

_____

2.

In the winter, _____

_____

3.

In the spring, _____

_____

4.

In the summer, _____

_____

Fruity Fun

Directions: Look at each picture. Write a subtraction problem to match the picture.

1.

☐ − ☐ = ☐

4.

☐ − ☐ = ☐

2.

☐ − ☐ = ☐

5.

☐ − ☐ = ☐

3.

☐ − ☐ = ☐

6.

☐ − ☐ = ☐

What Color Is It?

Directions: Read the sentences. Color the pictures to match.

The sun is **yellow**.

The grass is **green**.

The cat is **black**.

The bear is **brown**.

The heart is **red**.

The pumpkin is **orange**.

The bird is **blue**.

The hat is **black**.

Color the Robot

Directions:

✿ Color the ▢ s **red**.

✿ Color the ▭ s **blue**.

✿ Color the ◯ s **yellow**.

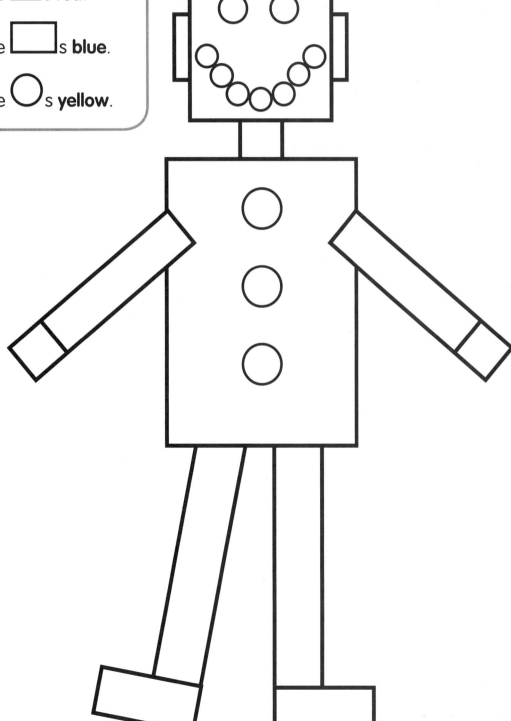

Lake Map

Directions: Look at the map of the lake. Follow the directions below.

1. Draw **green** paths from the mountain homes to the lake.
2. Draw **brown** paths from the lake homes to the trees.
3. Draw a **yellow** sun in the sky.
4. Draw a **red** boat in the lake.

Adding Doubles

Directions: Draw spots on the first wing of the butterfly to match the first number. Then, draw spots on the second wing to match the second number. How many spots are there altogether? Write the number in the boxes.

$$7 + 7 = \boxed{}$$

$$4 + 4 = \boxed{}$$

$$6 + 6 = \boxed{}$$

$$8 + 8 = \boxed{}$$

Shape Trace

Directions: Trace each shape and the shape word. Color each shape a different color.

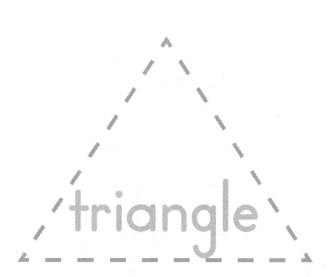

Number Patterns

Directions: Look at each line of number patterns. Write the missing number in the box to complete the pattern.

1   2   3   1   2   ☐

6   9   6   9   ☐   9

5   7   7   5   7   ☐

3   4   ☐   3   4   5

9   ☐   9   8   9   8

8   7   6   8   ☐   6

Happiness Is . . .

Directions: Draw two things that make you happy. Write a sentence about each one.

Uncrossed

Directions: Lightly color in squares to match the first number. Cross out squares to match the second number. How many squares are left uncrossed? Write this number in the circle.

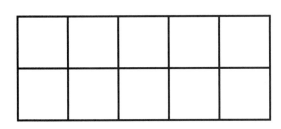

$10 - 7 =$ ◯

$10 - 9 =$ ◯

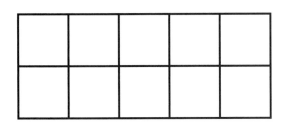

$10 - 6 =$ ◯

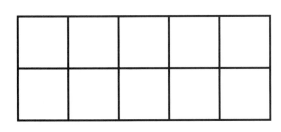

$10 - 8 =$ ◯

More Shape Trace

Directions: Trace each shape and the shape word. Color each shape a different color.

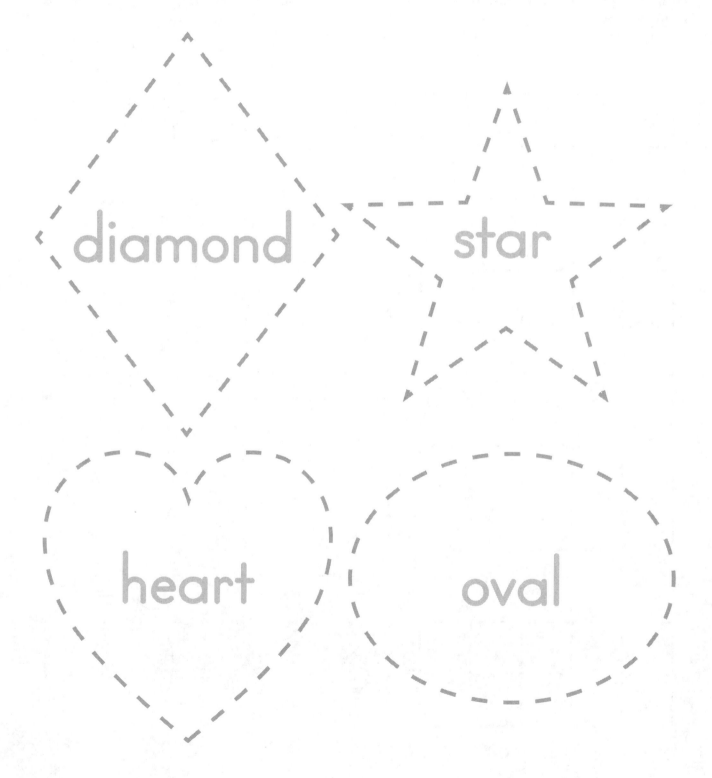

Boys and Girls

Directions: Count the boys on the bus, and graph the total. Then, count the girls on the bus, and graph the total. Color the bus.

boys			
girls			

SCHOOL BUS

Tan Ant

Directions: Write a story using the beginning below.

Last weekend, I went to the beach. I saw an ant sunbathing.

_____

- -

_____

- -

_____

- -

_____

- -

_____

- -

_____

Finding Patterns

Directions: Find the patterns in the picture. Color or circle the patterns.

Where Is the Ball?

Directions: Read the word on the left side. Look at where the ball is in each picture. Draw a line from the word to the picture that matches the word.

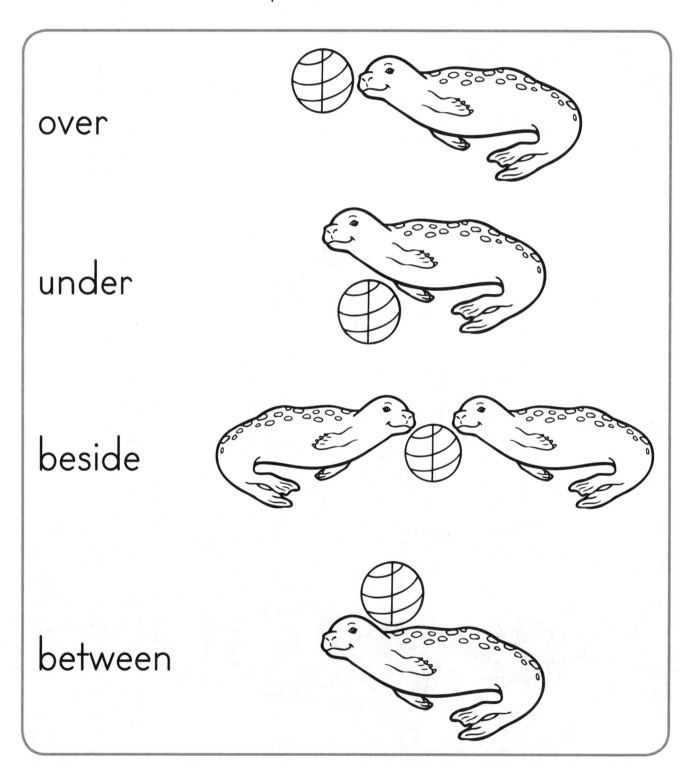

over

under

beside

between

Numbers 1 to 20

Week 8: Monday

Math

Directions: Trace the numbers from 1 to 20 in the first section. Write the numbers from 1 to 20 in the second section.

1	2	3	4	5
6	7	8	9	10
11	12	13	14	15
16	17	18	19	20

Cake Mix-Up

Directions: The pages of the story are mixed up. Read the story, and look at the pictures. Write the page numbers in the boxes.

I used pink frosting.

I added candy flowers.

I made a cake.

Dad lit the candle.

Tricky Patterns

Math

Directions: Using different-colored crayons, color the rows of pictures in each box to create the pattern shown.

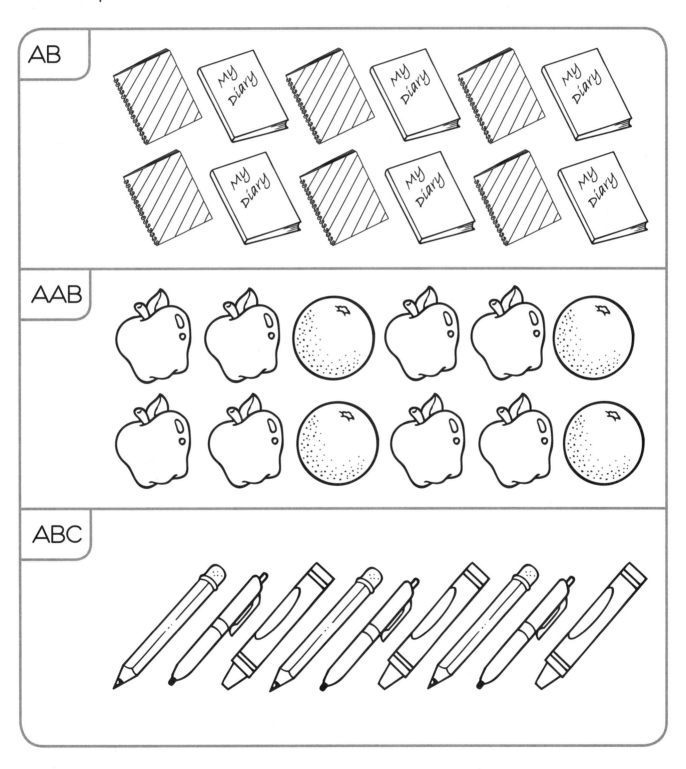

AB

AAB

ABC

How Many?

Directions: Read the sentences. Draw a picture to match each sentence.

Here are **two** ♡ s.

Here are **four** s.

Here is **one** .

Here are **six** s.

Here are **five** s.

Here are **three** s.

A Number of Steps

Directions: Write the missing numbers on the steps to show how you count from 10 to 20.

What Happened?

Directions: Look at the picture below. Write about what you think happened next.

Hot and Cold

Directions: The taller the line on a thermometer, the hotter the temperature. Color **red** the thermometer in each row that shows the hottest temperature. Color **blue** the thermometer in each row that shows the coldest temperature.

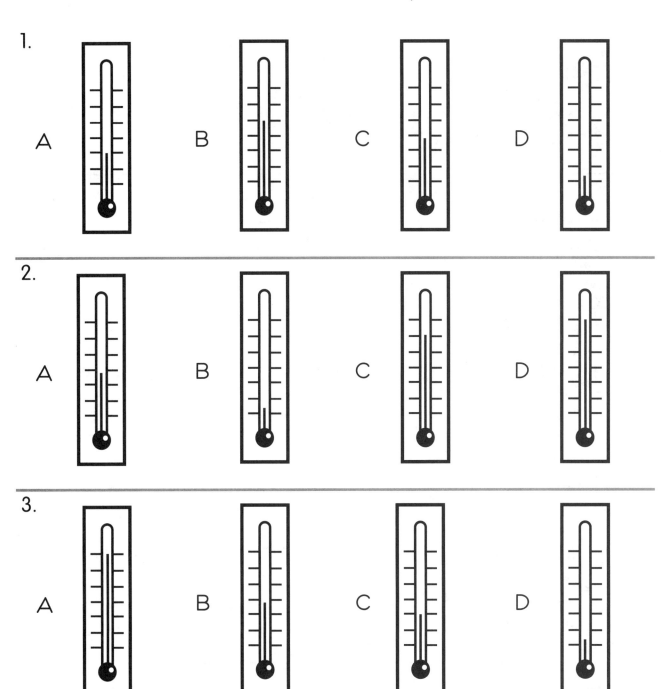

Zoo Beginnings

Directions: Say the name of each animal. Write the missing letter that represents its beginning sound. Trace the whole word.

1. _ebra_	2. _izard_	3. _angaroo_
4. _orse_	5. _iger_	6. _amel_
7. _alrus_	8. _nake_	9. _abbit_

Joining the Dots

Directions: Here is a hidden picture. What do you think it might be? Starting at 0, join the numbers from 0 to 20 to make the picture.

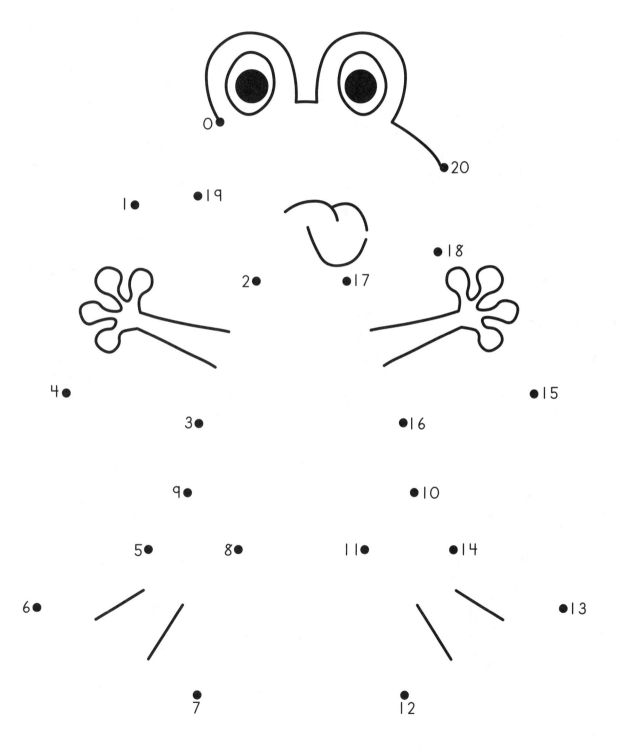

For Your Teeth

Directions: Put an **X** on the things that are bad for your teeth. Color the things that are good for your teeth.

More Friday Fun

The Friday Fun activities in this book are an entertaining way to wrap up a week of learning while still providing your child with enrichment in a variety of areas. In addition to the written activities provided, consider incorporating the following interactive games and activities to extend your child's learning beyond the page.

Week 1: Same and Different

Collect small groups of objects, such as toy cars, hair clips, shells, or socks. Look at the objects in one of the groups with your child. Ask how they are the same and how they are different. Encourage your child to compare other objects in the other groups.

Week 2: Blast Off

Play the *What's Different?* game with your child. Assemble a small group of objects, such as cooking utensils, small toys, or desk accessories, on a tray. Let your child study the group of objects for a minute. Then, have your child turn his or her back to the tray while you remove an object. See if your child can figure out what is different. Replace the object and repeat with a different object. Take turns removing objects.

Week 3: Pizza

Take your child to lunch at a pizza parlor where you can watch your pizza being made. Talk about the different food groups and about toppings you both like and dislike. Or make your own pizza at home. Have your child help create a shopping list of needed ingredients, go to the store with you to buy them, and make the pizza.

Week 4: Flower Needs

Visit a nursery to see the wide variety of plants and flowers that grow in your area. Buy some seeds or herbs to plant and grow. Put your child in charge of caring for the plants. Your child may want to keep a science journal to record his or her observations as the plants progress.

Week 5: Rhyme or Not?

After completing page 60, play the Rhyme Game. Pick a word, such as *mat, dog,* or *red,* and work together to list as many rhyming words as you can. Try this with other words. Then, visit your local library to find books that use rhyming words in stories or poems.

Week 6: Lake Map

Help your child make a map of his or her own. Consider making a map of your street or a favorite park. Look at and discuss different maps, such as road maps, amusement park maps, and globes.

Week 7: Where Is the Ball?

Hide a toy in the house or yard for your child to find. Give your child clues about where to find it using words that describe its location or position. (e.g., The teddy bear is next to something red.) Take turns hiding the toy and providing clues.

Week 8: For Your Teeth

Make arrangements to visit a dentist's office for a tour. Talk about how to keep teeth and gums healthy. Have your child brush his or her teeth. Then use a plaque-disclosing tablet (available from your dentist) to reveal the plaque still lurking in his or her mouth. Practice brushing to remove the plaque.

All About Me

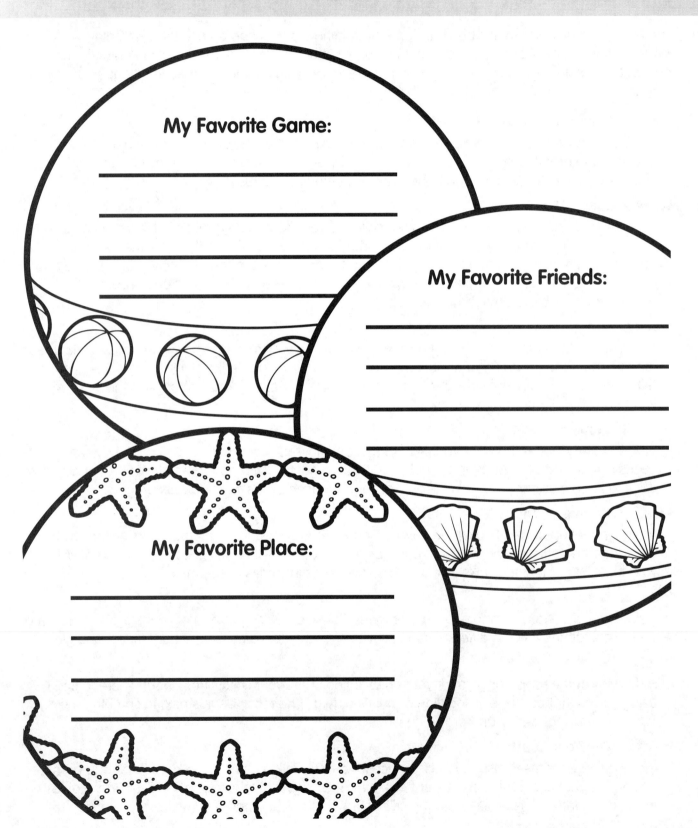

My Favorite Game:

_____

_____

_____

_____

My Favorite Friends:

_____

_____

_____

My Favorite Place:

_____

_____

_____

Fun Ways to Love Books

Here are some fun ways that your child can expand on his or her reading. Most of these ideas will involve both you and your child; however, the wording has been directed towards your child because we want him or her to be inspired to love books.

Design a Bookmark

You can design a bookmark for your favorite book, and then use it in other books to remind you of a great reading experience. Use a strip of colorful paper and include the title, the author, and a picture of something that happened in the book.

Book Chain

Create a book chain to link your favorite books together. First, cut out strips of colored paper. On one strip, write down the name of your favorite book. On the other, describe your favorite part of the story. Staple or tape the strips of paper together to form a circle. Do this for each book you read, and link all of your books together. Use the chain to decorate your room.

A Comic Book

Turn your favorite book into a comic book. Fold at least two sheets of paper in half, and staple them so they make a book. With a ruler and pencil, draw boxes across each page to look like blank comic strips. Then, draw the story of your book as if it were a comic. Draw pictures of your characters, and have words coming out of their mouths—just as in a real comic strip.

Always Take a Book

Maybe you've had to wait with your parents in line at the post office or in the vet's waiting room with nothing to do. If you get into the habit of bringing a book with you wherever you go, you'll always have something exciting to do! Train yourself to always take a good book. You might want to carry a small backpack or shoulder bag—something that allows you to carry a book easily from place to place. Don't forget a bookmark!

Learn a New Skill

What skills are mentioned in your favorite book? Perhaps a character learns to ride a unicycle. Other characters may create beautiful pottery, learn to juggle, take black-and-white photographs, train dogs, or bake five-layer cakes. Identify a skill mentioned in your book. Gather together the materials you'll need to learn this skill. Keep in mind that learning a new skill may take several weeks or months. Commit to practicing this skill at least twice a week. Keep a journal detailing your growing abilities. Finally, organize a talent show to demonstrate your newfound skill!

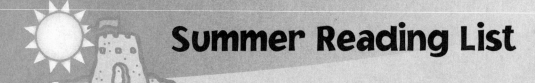

Summer Reading List

✿ **Song and Dance Man** by Karen Ackerman
A grandfather recalls his vaudeville days as he entertains his grandchildren.

✿ **Cloudy with a Chance of Meatballs** by Judi Barrett
Everything is great in the town of Chewandswallow, where it rains food three times a day, until the portions get bigger.

✿ **Stone Soup** by Marsha Brown
Three hungry soldiers trick a town into making a delicious feast for them.

✿ **I Like Me!** by Nancy Carlson
This story about a pig encourages children to like themselves and take good care of themselves.

✿ **Truck** by Donald Crews
Children can make up their own stories as they follow a big, red truck on its wordless journey.

✿ **Olivia** by Ian Falconer
Meet Olivia, a precocious, high-energy pig, in her first book of many.

✿ **If You Give a Mouse a Cookie** by Laura Joffe Numeroff
One thing leads to another after a boy shares a cookie with a mouse.

✿ **Leo the Late Bloomer** by Robert Kraus
Leo, the tiger, can't do everything his friends can, but his mom isn't worried. She knows he'll catch up in his own time.

✿ **Bats at the Library** by Brian Lies
This library adventure combines the love of reading with the love of bats that take on human qualities and actions.

✿ **Fables** by Arnold Lobel
This book provides a great collection of fables.

✿ **Barn Dance!** by Bill Martin Jr.
While the farmer sleeps, the animals gather in the barn to kick up their hooves as the scarecrow plays his fiddle.

Making the Most of Summertime Reading

When reading these books with your child, you may wish to ask the questions below. The sharing of questions and answers will enhance and improve your child's reading comprehension skills.

✿ Why did you pick this book to read?

✿ Name a character from the story that you like. Why do you like him or her?

✿ Where does the story take place? Do you want to go there?

✿ Name a problem from the story. How is it solved?

✿ What is the best part of the story so far? Describe it!

✿ What do you think is going to happen next in the story? Guess!

✿ Who are the important characters in the story? Why are they important?

✿ What is the book about?

✿ What are two things you have learned by reading this book?

✿ Would you tell your friend to read this book? Why or why not?

Summer Reading List
(cont.)

- **Mary Wore Her Red Dress and Henry Wore His Green Sneakers** by Merle Peek

  Everyone is excited about the birthday party, so they dress their best in an array of colors.

- **The Kissing Hand** by Audrey Penn

  When a little raccoon is nervous about going to school, his mother finds a way to soothe his worries away.

- **We're Going on a Bear Hunt** by Michael Rosen

  Based on the familiar chant, a father and his children go on a bear hunt.

- **Where the Wild Things Are** by Maurice Sendak

  After being sent to his room without dinner, a boy finds himself on an interesting adventure among the wild things.

- **Sheep in a Jeep** by Nancy E. Shaw

  Five foolish sheep in a jeep head off on a rhyming road trip.

- **I'm the Best Artist in the Ocean** by Kevin Sherry

  In this undersea adventure, a giant blue squid is challenging the art world with his creative masterpieces.

- **The Stray Dog** by Marc Simont

  This story is about a stray dog that is befriended by two children who meet him at the park.

- **Sylvester and the Magic Pebble** by William Steig

  Sylvester finds a magic pebble that makes all his wishes come true, but when he encounters a lion, he makes an unfortunate wish that separates him from his family. What will he do?

- **Have You Seen My Duckling?** by Nancy Tafuri

  Mother duck can't find her duckling, even though he is hidden on every page.

- **Alexander and the Terrible, Horrible, No Good, Very Bad Day** by Judith Viorst

  Everyone has bad days, but Alexander's is so bad that he wants to "move to Australia."

- **Jesse Bear, What Will You Wear?** by Nancy White Carlstrom

  Jesse Bear wears a variety of things, not just clothes, throughout the day in this rhyming tale.

- **The Pigeon Wants a Puppy** by Mo Willems

  A bird insists on getting a puppy as a pet. He promises to take care of it, but will this be enough for him to get the puppy?

- **The Night Before Kindergarten** by Natasha Wing

  Get ready for kindergarten with this clever twist on Clement C. Moore's classic Christmas poem.

- **Goodnight Moon** by Margaret Wise Brown

  In charming, poetic verse, a little bunny says goodnight.

Bookmark Your Words

Make summertime reading lots of fun with these reading log glasses. Have your child fill in the glasses after his or her daily reading. For younger children, you may need to help them fill in the information. Or, as an alternative, they can draw a picture of something they read from that day. Once they have completed the glasses, they can cut them out and use them as bookmarks.

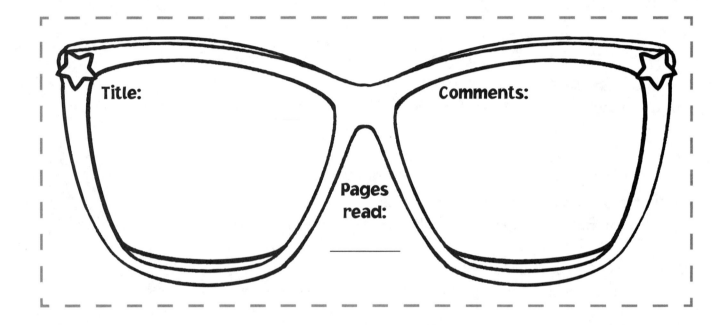

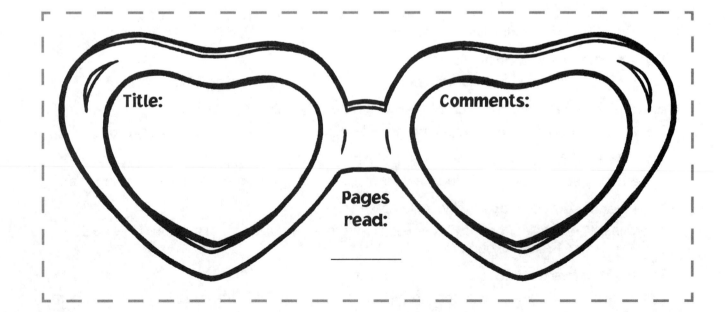

This page may be reproduced as many times as needed.

Read-Together Chart

Does your father read books to you before bed? Perhaps your mother reads to the family at breakfast? Your grandparents may enjoy reading books to you after school or on the weekends. You and your family members can create a Read-Together Chart and fill it in to keep track of all the books you've read together.

Here are two Read-Together Charts. The first one is a sample. The second one has been left blank, so you can add your own categories and books.

Sample Chart

Book We Read	Who Read It?	Summary	Our Review
The Secret Garden	My older sister read it to me.	It's about a spoiled girl who learns to love nature and people.	We like this book. The characters are funny, and the illustrations are beautiful!

Your Chart

This page may be reproduced as many times as needed.

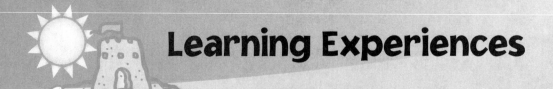

Learning Experiences

Here are some fun, low-cost activities that you can do with your child. You'll soon discover that these activities can be stimulating, educational, and complementary to the other exercises in this book.

Flash Cards

Make up all types of flash cards. Depending on your child's interest and grade level, these cards might feature enrichment words, math problems, or states and capitals. You can create them yourself with markers or on a computer. Let your child help cut pictures out of magazines and glue them on. Then, find a spot outdoors, and go through the flash cards with your child.

Project Pantry

Find a spot in your house where you can store supplies. This might be a closet or a bin that stays in one spot. Get some clean paint cans or buckets. Fill them with all types of craft and art supplies. Besides the typical paints, markers, paper, scissors, and glue, include some more unusual things, such as tiles, artificial flowers, and wrapping paper. This way, whenever you and your child want to do a craft project, you have everything you need at that moment.

The Local Library

Check out everything that your local library has to offer. Most libraries offer summer reading programs with various incentives. Spend an afternoon choosing and then reading books together.

Collect Something

Let your child choose something to collect that is free or inexpensive, such as paper clips or buttons. If your child wants to collect something that might be impractical, like horses, find pictures in magazines or catalogs, and have your child cut them out and start a picture collection.

Grocery Store Trip

Instead of making a trip to the grocery store a chore, make it a challenge. Even with nonreaders, you can have them help you find items on the shelf. Start by giving your child a list of his or her own. Review the list before you go. For nonreaders, you might want to cut pictures from ads. Many stores even have smaller shopping carts, so your child can have his or her own cart to fill. Once you get to an aisle where you know there is something on your child's list, prompt him or her to find the item. You may have to help your child get something down from a shelf.

Eating the Alphabet

Wouldn't it be fun to eat the alphabet? During the course of the summer, see how many fresh fruits and vegetables you can eat from A to Z. You and your child can make a poster or a chart with the letters A–Z on it. Once you have the chart, each time your child eats a fruit or vegetable, write it next to the matching letter of the alphabet. You can also let your child draw a picture of what he or she has eaten.

How Much Does It Cost?

If you go out for a meal, have your child help total the bill. Write down the cost of each person's meal. Then, have your child add them all together. You can vary this and make it much simpler by having your child just figure out the cost of an entrée and a drink or the cost of three desserts. You might want to round the figures first.

Nature Scavenger Hunt

Take a walk, go to a park, or hike in the mountains. But before you go, create a scavenger hunt list for your child. This can consist of all sorts of things found in nature. Make sure your child has a bag to carry everything he or she finds. (Be sure to check ahead of time about the rules or laws regarding removing anything.) You might include things like a leaf with pointed edges, a speckled rock, and a twig with two small limbs on it. Take a few minutes to look at all the things your child has collected, and check them off the list.

Measure It!

Using a ruler, tape measure, or yardstick is one way to see how tall something is. Start with your child, and find out how tall he or she is. Now find other things to measure and compare. Find out how much shorter a book is compared to your child, or discover how much taller the door is than your child. To measure things that can't be measured with a ruler, take some string and stretch it around the object. Cut or mark it where it ends. Then, stretch the string next to the ruler or tape measure to find out how long it is. Your child may be surprised at how different something that is the same number of inches looks when the shape is different.

Take a Trip, and Keep a Journal

If you are going away during the summer, have your child keep a journal. Depending on his or her age, this can take a different look. A young child can collect postcards and paste them into a blank journal. He or she can also draw pictures of places he or she is visiting. An older child can keep a traditional journal and draw pictures. Your child can also do a photo-journal if a camera is available for him or her to use.

Be a Scientist

Without your child's knowledge, put a ball inside a box, and cover it with a lid. Call in your child, and tell him or her to act like a scientist. He or she will need to ask questions and try to figure out answers like a scientist would. If your child is having a hard time asking questions, you may need to help. Some questions to ask include, "What do you think is inside the box?" and "How do you know?" Have your child shake the box and see if he or she can figure it out.

Journal Topics

Choose one of these journal topics each day. Make sure you add enough detail so someone else reading this will clearly be able to know at least four of the following:

☼ **who**　　☼ **what**　　☼ **when**　　☼ **where**　　☼ **why**　　☼ **how**

1. My favorite thing to do in the summer is . . .
2. A toy that I want is . . .
3. On a rainy day, I wear . . .
4. An animal I like is . . .
5. I am scared of . . .
6. My favorite place to eat is . . .
7. My room is . . .
8. My favorite book is . . .
9. I get ready for school . . .
10. I want to travel to . . .
11. On my last birthday, I . . .
12. My favorite holiday is . . .
13. When I am happy, I . . .
14. A food I like to eat is . . .
15. My favorite color is . . .
16. The weather today is . . .
17. My favorite person is . . .
18. An ice-cream flavor I like is . . .
19. During the weekend, I like to . . .
20. My favorite superhero is . . .
21. I usually remember to . . .
22. I like to talk to . . .
23. I get mad when . . .
24. I always forget to . . .
25. I like to draw . . .

Web Sites

Math Web Sites

☼ **AAA Math:** http://www.aaamath.com
This site contains hundreds of pages of basic math skills divided by grade or topic.

☼ **AllMath.com:** http://www.allmath.com
This site has math flashcards, biographies of mathematicians, and a math glossary.

☼ **BrainBashers:** http://www.brainbashers.com
This is a unique collection of brainteasers, games, and optical illusions.

☼ **Coolmath.com:** http://www.coolmath.com
Explore this amusement park of mathematics! Have fun with the interactive activities.

☼ **Mrs. Glosser's Math Goodies:** http://www.mathgoodies.com
This is a free educational Web site featuring interactive worksheets, puzzles, and more!

Reading and Writing Web Sites

☼ **Aesop's Fables:** http://www.umass.edu/aesop
This site has almost forty of the fables. Both traditional and modern versions are presented.

☼ **American Library Association:** http://ala.org
Visit this site to find out both the past and present John Newbery Medal and Randolph Caldecott Medal winners.

☼ **Book Adventure:** http://www.bookadventure.com
This site features a free reading incentive program dedicated to encouraging children in grades K–8 to read.

☼ **Chateau Meddybemps—Young Writers Workshop:** http://www.meddybemps.com/9.700.html
Use the provided story starters to help your child write a story.

☼ **Fairy Godmother:** http://www.fairygodmother.com
This site will capture your child's imagination and spur it on to wonderful creativity.

☼ **Grammar Gorillas:** http://www.funbrain.com/grammar
Play grammar games on this site that proves that grammar can be fun!

☼ **Graphic Organizers:** http://www.eduplace.com/graphicorganizer
Use these graphic organizers to help your child write in an organized manner.

☼ **Rhymezone:** http://www.rhymezone.com
Type in the word you want to rhyme. If there is a rhyming word to match your word, you'll find it here.

☼ **Storybook:** http://www.kids-space.org/story/story.html
Storybook takes children's stories and publishes them on this Web site. Just like in a library, children can choose a shelf and read stories.

Web Sites *(cont.)*

Reading and Writing Web Sites *(cont.)*

☼ **Wacky Web Tales:** http://www.eduplace.com/tales/index.html
This is a great place for budding writers to submit their stories and read other children's writing.

☼ **Write on Reader:** http://library.thinkquest.org/J001156
Children can visit Write on Reader to gain a love of reading and writing.

General Web Sites

☼ **Animal Photos:** http://nationalzoo.si.edu
This site offers wonderful pictures of animals, as well as virtual zoo visits.

☼ **Congress for Kids:** http://www.congressforkids.net
Children can go to this site to learn all about the branches of the United States Government.

☼ **Dinosaur Guide:** http://dsc.discovery.com/dinosaurs
This is an interactive site on dinosaurs that goes beyond just learning about the creatures.

☼ **The Dinosauria:** http://www.ucmp.berkeley.edu/diapsids/dinosaur.html
This site focuses on dispelling dinosaur myths. Read about fossils, history, and more.

☼ **Earthquake Legends:** http://www.fema.gov/kids/eqlegnd.htm
On this site, children can read some of the tales behind earthquakes that people of various cultures once believed.

☼ **The Electronic Zoo:** http://netvet.wustl.edu/e-zoo.htm
This site has links to thousands of animal sites covering every creature under the sun!

☼ **Great Buildings Online:** http://www.greatbuildings.com
This gateway to architecture around the world and across history documents a thousand buildings and hundreds of leading architects.

☼ **Maggie's Earth Adventures:** http://www.missmaggie.org
Join Maggie and her dog, Dude, on a wonderful Earth adventure.

☼ **Mr. Dowling's Electronic Passport:** http://www.mrdowling.com/index.html
This is an incredible history and geography site.

☼ **Sesame Street:** http://www.sesamestreet.org
There is no shortage of fun for children at Sesame Street.

☼ **Tropical Twisters:** http://kids.mtpe.hq.nasa.gov/archive/hurricane/index.html
Take an in-depth look at hurricanes, from how they're created to how dangerous they are.

Printing Chart

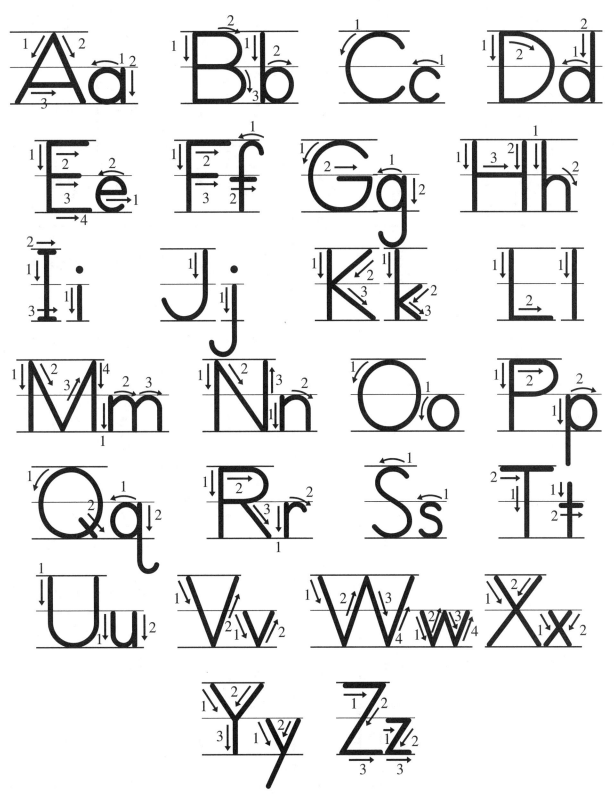

numbers 1–100

1	2	3	4	5	6	7	8	9	10
11	12	13	14	15	16	17	18	19	20
21	22	23	24	25	26	27	28	29	30
31	32	33	34	35	36	37	38	39	40
41	42	43	44	45	46	47	48	49	50
51	52	53	54	55	56	57	58	59	60
61	62	63	64	65	66	67	68	69	70
71	72	73	74	75	76	77	78	79	80
81	82	83	84	85	86	87	88	89	90
91	92	93	94	95	96	97	98	99	100

Addition Chart

+	0	1	2	3	4	5	6	7	8	9
0	0	1	2	3	4	5	6	7	8	9
1	1	2	3	4	5	6	7	8	9	10
2	2	3	4	5	6	7	8	9	10	11
3	3	4	5	6	7	8	9	10	11	12
4	4	5	6	7	8	9	10	11	12	13
5	5	6	7	8	9	10	11	12	13	14
6	6	7	8	9	10	11	12	13	14	15
7	7	8	9	10	11	12	13	14	15	16
8	8	9	10	11	12	13	14	15	16	17
9	9	10	11	12	13	14	15	16	17	18

Money Chart

penny	
1¢ 1 cent $0.01	● ● ● ● ● ● ● ● ● ● = ●

nickel	
5¢ 5 cents $0.05	● ● ● ● ● = ●

dime	
10¢ 10 cents $0.10	● ● ● ● ● = ●

quarter	
25¢ 25 cents $0.25	● ● ● ● = THE UNITED STATES ONE DOLLAR

half dollar	
50¢ 50 cents $0.50	● ● = THE UNITED STATES ONE DOLLAR

dollar	
THE UNITED STATES ONE DOLLAR =	100 pennies 20 nickels 10 dimes 4 quarters 2 half dollars

Answer Key

Page 11

0	☆☆☆☆☆☆☆☆☆☆
1	★☆☆☆☆☆☆☆☆☆
2	★★☆☆☆☆☆☆☆☆
3	★★★☆☆☆☆☆☆☆
4	★★★★☆☆☆☆☆☆
5	★★★★★☆☆☆☆☆
6	★★★★★★☆☆☆☆
7	★★★★★★★☆☆☆
8	★★★★★★★★☆☆
9	★★★★★★★★★☆
10	★★★★★★★★★★

Page 12

1. ball, bee
2. leaf, lion
3. monkey, man
4. rabbit, rainbow
5. sun, six

Page 13

houses: 5

nails: 7

hard hats: 3

hammers: 6

wrenches: 8

trash cans: 2

Page 14

C, D, F, I, K, L, N, R, S, T, V, X, Y

Page 15

1, 5, 6, 7

2, 3, 4, 8

4, 6, 8, 9

Page 16

1. c
2. b
3. l
4. m
5. t
6. r
7. s
8. f
9. w

Page 17

Each animal should have the same number of spots as written beside it.

Page 18

Answers will vary.

Page 19

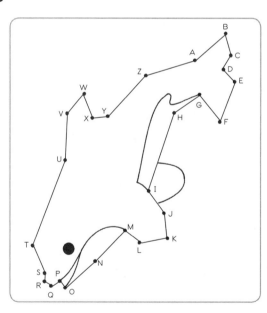

Page 20

☼ Color the two plain hot-fudge sundaes, and cross out the sundae with a cherry.

☼ Color the two, two-holed buttons, and cross out the four-holed button.

☼ Color the two freckled dogs, and cross out the dog without freckles.

☼ Color the two glue bottles, and cross out the blank bottle.

Answer Key (cont.)

Page 21

1. Put an **X** on the circle.

2. Put an **X** on the triangle.

3. Put an **X** on the diamond.

4. Put an **X** on the square.

Page 22

b, e, f, h, i, l, m, n, o, q, s, t, u, w, x, z

Page 23

1. 8

2. 9

3. 7

4. 12

5. 10

6. 6

7. 5

8. 11

Page 24

○ Circle the flies, frog, fish, and fox.

○ Draw a box around the raccoon, rat, and rabbit.

○ Place an **X** over the skunk, snake, spider, and snail.

Page 25

○ Circle the ice-cream cone, milk, drink, hot dog, sandwich, and carrots.

○ Draw a square around the taco, hamburger, corn, chips, pizza slice, and soda.

Page 26

Answers will vary.

Page 27

cars:	4	hills:	3
trees:	5	houses:	1
trucks:	2	rabbits:	4

Page 28

1. **t**op, **t**ub, **t**ire

2. **b**ag, **b**ell, **b**all

3. **r**ing, **r**ug, **r**ock

4. **p**ig, **p**ot, **p**en

Page 29

the bird's second wing, the giraffe's tail, the rhino's horn, the dog's ears, the kangaroo's eye, and the gorilla's mouth

Page 30

Circle the flames, left wing, cargo doors, and nose in the second picture.

Page 31

1. Color "C" yellow, and cross out "B."

2. Color "A" yellow, and cross out "B."

3. Color "A" yellow, and cross out "C."

Page 32

1. ax, box

2. bag, dog

3. can, sun

4. cat, bat

5. gum, broom

Page 33

Each fish should have the same number of bubbles as written beside it.

Page 34

Answers will vary.

Page 35

1. heart

2. triangle

3. heart

4. triangle

5. square

Answer Key *(cont.)*

Page 36
1. tub
2. bucket
3. duck
4. sun
5. can

Page 37
Guesses will vary.
1. 3
2. 4
3. 5
4. 6
5. 7
6. 9

Page 38
Flower: 3, 2, 1
Sandcastle: 2, 1, 3
Snowman: 1, 2, 3

Page 39
Answers will vary.

Page 40

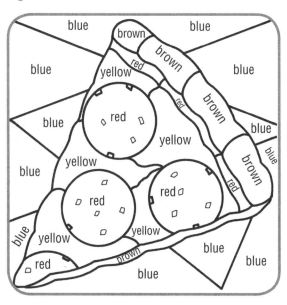

Page 41
1. 5
2. 3
3. 5
4. 5
5. 6
6. 6
7. 4
8. 4

Page 42
Ff, Kk, Mm, Bb, Ee, Gg, Tt, Hh, Nn, Rr

Page 43
pitcher A, cup C, bucket D, box B

Page 44
1. sun, sub
2. pig, pin
3. web, wet
4. cat, can
5. dog, dot
6. bag, bat

Page 45
3 + 5 = **8**
1 + 4 = **5**
4 + 3 = **7**

Page 46
Answers will vary.

Page 47
☼ Circle the rabbits column.
☼ Color the dogs column blue.
☼ Color the cats column yellow.

Page 50
☼ Color the water, dirt, and sun.
☼ Draw an **X** on the wind, apple, ice skate, and watch.

Answer Key (cont.)

Page 51

1. 2
2. 3
3. 1
4. 1
5. 1
6. 2

Page 52

All of the foods start with the letter "b."

Page 53

1. M, S, L
2. S, L, M
3. M, L, S

Page 54

Answers will vary.

Page 55

1. 3
2. 2
3. 2
4. 1
5. 1
6. 3

Page 56

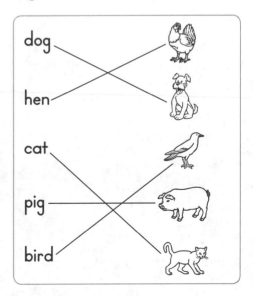

Page 57

triangles: 10

hexagons: 5

squares: 4

Page 58

Answers will vary.

Page 59

Answers will vary.

Page 60

1. rhyme (smiley face)
2. rhyme (smiley face)
3. do not rhyme (sad face)
4. rhyme (smiley face)
5. do not rhyme (sad face)
6. rhyme (smiley face)

Page 61

$5 + 5 = 10$

$2 + 8 = 10$

$6 + 4 = 10$

$10 + 0 = 10$

Page 62

Answers will vary.

Page 63

1. Flowers: 2 (less), 3 (more)
2. Apples: 7 (more), 6 (less)
3. Mushrooms: 10 (more), 7 (less)
4. Dots: 5 (less), 8 (more)

Page 64

1. cat
2. cot
3. hug
4. hog
5. fan

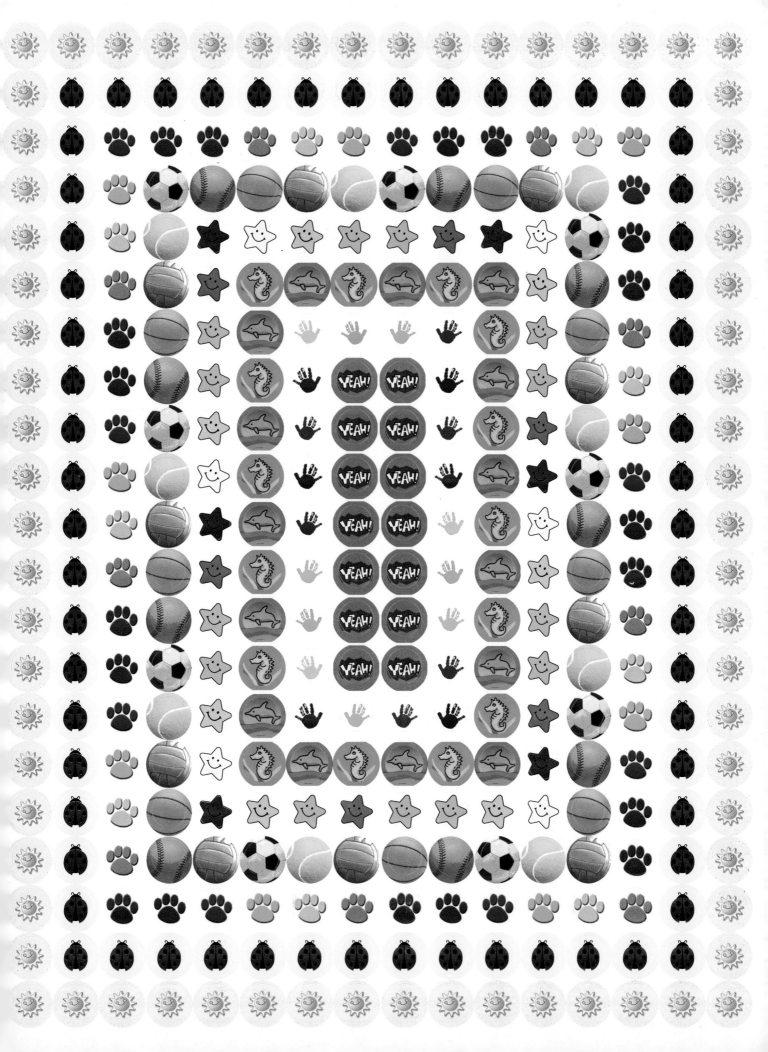